Kids' Questions about Church and the Future

Cheryl Fawcett
Robert C. Newman

Illustrations by Ron Mazellan

Regular Baptist Press
1300 North Meacham Road
Schaumburg, Illinois 60173

To Joyce Tepfer, the director of children's ministry at Shadow Mountain High Kids ministry in El Cajon, California. Your endless energy, creativity, abounding love, and sacrificial life to minister to nearly 400 volunteers and 1,000 children a week spurs me on to be my best for God!—Cheryl Fawcett

To Pastor Douglas Christen, who introduced me to Christ as a senior in high school and helped to change the direction of my life and work. In high school Bob Newman ran cross-country; in his life he ran the race of faith. And now he has completed his course. He faithfully kept the faith and is now enjoying his runner's crown—along with the apostle Paul and others who have gone before.—Betty Newman for Bob

KIDS' QUESTIONS ABOUT CHURCH AND THE FUTURE
© 2003, 1994 (formerly published as part of *I Have a Question about God*)
Regular Baptist Press • Schaumburg, Illinois
1-800-727-4400 • www.regularbaptistpress.org
Printed in U.S.A.
All rights reserved
RBP5307 • ISBN: 1-59402-084-1

Contents

Preface

God has used church families throughout my life to mold my faith, my life, and my dreams. I was baptized into Capital Baptist Church in Washington, D.C., when I was seven years old. That family of believers forged my faith until I left for college. Heritage Baptist Church in Clarks Summit, Pennsylvania, provided my first opportunities to teach children doctrine. Faith Baptist Church in Winfield, Illinois, formed my ministry skills. Tabernacle Baptist Church in Ithaca, New York, refined my teaching to non-churched children through released time classes. Springville Baptist Church in Springville, Pennsylvania, reminded me that children love stories, as I taught children's corner for nearly ten years. Shawnee Hills Baptist Church in Jamestown, Ohio, stretched me as I taught young children doctrine, assisted by my collegiate advisees.

Wherever I meet children or adults, they are sinners who need a Savior. The same truth applies to all. And the same hope in Christ is available to all. The return of Jesus is very soon. We must be ready to meet Him.

Kids' Questions about Church

Hints and Helps

S ome Christians don't think much of the local church. These people gather in all kinds of Christian groups outside the church, but seldom are they loyal to a local church. They are something like the world traveler who never got to know his own family.

When we speak of church, we might refer to the "universal church," which includes all the people (from Acts 2 until the coming Rapture) who have confessed their sins and embraced Christ as Savior. Although the universal church is real, we cannot see it. If I am hurt, I cannot go to the universal church for consolation. If I need counsel, I can't speak with the pastor of the church universal, as there is no such person. Thus "church" primarily refers to a local body of believers, of which we all need to be a part.

The church is people who love God and who have admitted their need of His saving work in their lives. The local church is also made up of leaders and officers, beginning with the pastor. The Bible likens believers to sheep and the pastor to a shepherd who oversees the flock.

In the book of Ephesians Paul used three illustrations to teach us what constitutes the universal church. First, Ephesians 1:22 and 23 refer to the church as a body. Every body has a head, or center of control. Christ serves as the head of the church body.

Second, in Ephesians 2:19–22, Paul described the church as a building. A building has a foundation, and the church has its foundation— the apostles and prophets. Under the inspiration of God, they wrote the instruction manual, the Bible, for the church. This analogy of a building describes Christ as the chief cornerstone. In ancient Middle Eastern times, buildings were designed so that a chief cornerstone held a whole building together. If someone were to remove the chief cornerstone, the entire building would fall apart. Likewise, Christ is central, or integral, to the church. Without Him it would dissolve into nothingness.

The third analogy in Ephesians 5:22–33 pictures the church as a bride, the wife of Christ. Christ serves as the bridegroom, or husband. The church is to be subject to Christ. Christ as the husband loves the church. He gave Himself for her.

A local, visible church should represent Christ and the universal church in a community. It should stand as a lighthouse of the gospel for people who need Christ. Furthermore, the local church should be a vital place of communion, fellowship, and instruction.

As we read the book of Ephesians, we understand that Christ loves His church—and we should too. We should submit to its leadership, love and aid in its ministry, and help advance the cause of Christ through it.

Verse to Memorize

Ephesians 5:25: "Christ also loved the church, and gave himself for it."

What Is That Building with the Spike?

Hi! My name is Topher. Really my name is Christopher, but my friends call me Toph or Topher. I'm eight. I like to ride my bike and play T-ball, soccer, and basketball. I have two sisters, Megan and Bobbie. Megan is ten and plays the piano all the time. She takes lessons. Roberta is four. We call her Bobbie. She's fun to tease, but she drives me nuts, always asking, "What's that?" or "What does this mean?" Mom and Dad say she'll grow out of always asking questions, but I doubt it.

Megan, Bobbie, Mom, and I were on our way to the library when Bobbie asked one of her famous questions. Well, at least they're famous in the Schmidt family.

"Mom, what's that building with the point over there?"

By the time Mom could see where Bobbie was pointing, we had passed the building. "That's okay, Mom. There are lots of those pointy things around. I'll show you a different one."

"What pointy things are you talking about, Bobbie? Do you mean a spike?"

Megan was acting really smart that day. School had gotten out just a few days before, and she had won an award for being the best student in her class.

Mom was trying to remember the buildings they had just passed. "Do you mean the museum?" she asked Bobbie.

"No, the fancy one with the poi—spike! Sometimes the spikes have sticks on top, but sometimes they don't. Sometimes they have windows, and sometimes they don't have windows." Bobbie was trying to explain the buildings, but it wasn't helping Mom. "There's another one, Mom, right there." Bobbie pointed out the window again.

Mom couldn't look that time. "Bobbie, I want to answer your question, but you keep waiting until we've passed the building before you point it out to me. Remember that I'm driving and need to look out the front window to keep the car moving safely."

Bobbie kept staring out the window. She pointed out the next pointy thing sooner. "There's another one, Mom. What's that spike thing?"

Mom finally saw one. "Oh, that's a church steeple. It's tall and white and points to the sky to remind people that God is much greater, higher, and holier than we. The sticks are actually a cross. Some churches have a cross there to remind people that Jesus died on the cross to pay for our sins. The windows are just to make it pretty."

"Does a church have to have a steekle?"

"It's 'steeple,' not 'steekle,' Bobbie, and many churches don't have steeples. Some churches don't even have buildings. In parts of Africa and South America, people love God and belong to His church without having a building of any kind. Some places have warm weather all year, so buildings aren't as important there. The people who love God just have a special meeting time when they all get together. It's fine to have a fancy building to remind us how beautiful and big God is, but that doesn't make a church. People do. You only have to have people who love God and have asked Jesus to save them from their sins to have a church."

The children were quiet for two whole blocks. That's a long time for them. Then Megan asked, "Does everyone at church love God? What about the people who don't know about Him but want to learn?"

"Anyone is welcome to go to church—the building or the meeting. Church is a great place to learn about God. In fact, many people who just visit eventually decide to be in God's family."

That night at dinner, Dad asked what the children had done that day. He asks them that all the time. Megan told him about the talk they had had about spikes and churches and God's family.

Then Bobbie asked some questions. "Dad, are you in that family? Am I in the family? Am I the church?"

"Bobbie, I'll have to think about that and answer you later. I have been thinking about some of those things for a while now. Maybe it's time to make up my mind. I think maybe we'll visit the 'spike place' this Sunday."

Verse to Memorize

Acts 2:47: "And the Lord added to the church daily such as should be saved."

QUESTIONS TO ASK YOUR CHILD

*

1. Why do steeples point to the sky?

2. What is a church?

3. Are you a part of the church?

Who Is the Man Standing behind the Box up Front?

Bobbie woke up early! The night before she had gotten out her best dress, her good shoes, and her socks that have lace on them. She got dressed and tiptoed into Mom and Dad's room. "Dad, is it time to go yet?"

"Bobbie, it's only 5:30! We don't have to get up till seven. Please go back to bed. I'll make sure you're up in time."

Bobbie went back to her room and took off her fancy clothes. She was quiet, but she was excited because they were going to visit the church with the spike.

After Dad had gotten Toph up, he went to Bobbie's room and told her it was time to get going. Bobbie practically jumped out of bed. She even beat Toph getting ready. She brought her Bible to the kitchen for breakfast.

When Bobbie, Megan, Mom and Dad, and Toph were in the car on their way to the church, Bobbie stared out the window. Then she yelled, "There's the spike!" when she saw it from blocks away above the treetops.

Megan had to tell her the right word. "Bobbie, it's a steeple, and please try to keep your questions to yourself today." Megan told Toph she was afraid Bobbie would say something dumb in front of everybody at the church.

Two men shook their hands when they walked into the church. The men seemed pretty nice. They said, "Hello! Thank you for coming!" One of them pointed the family to a big room with long wooden seats with ends on them. Mom said they're called pews. The man even helped them find a place to sit. The room was kind of pretty if you like fancy lights and colored windows.

Bobbie had to sit between Mom and Dad. "Mom, there's a piano like Megan plays." Then she crawled onto Dad's lap. "Dad, what's that big box up there?"

Megan was embarrassed. "Shhh, Bobbie. This is church, and you're supposed to be quiet!"

Dad told Megan he would take care of things. Then he answered Bobbie's question. "That's an organ. It plays beautiful music."

"Why?"

"Well . . . umm . . . the music helps you think about how big and mighty God really is. Listen, the lady is beginning to play the organ."

All the people in the church got really quiet when the lady played the organ, and everyone stayed quiet when she was done—everyone except Bobbie. She got off Dad's lap and got onto Mom's. In a super loud whisper, she asked, "Mom, who's that man behind the box up front? What's he doing with the big book?" Toph looked at Megan and rolled his eyes. Megan slid down in the seat, but Mom and Dad seemed happy that Bobbie wanted to know what was going on.

Mom told her that it was the pastor. "He has the Bible with him.

He'll read it out loud later this morning. The pastor is the leader of
the church. Sometimes he's called a shepherd. I'll tell you more when
we get home. Let's listen now, okay?"

Bobbie seemed to love church. The organ music was beautiful like

Dad said. She liked the people up front who sang a special song. She really liked the sheepherder man who Mom said they would talk about later.

After a while a man said, "We'll dismiss the children at this time." A bunch of kids got up and started to leave. Dad whispered to Toph that he and Megan and Bobbie could go with the other kids, so they followed them to a big room downstairs.

Bobbie went to one place for children. Megan and Toph went to a different place for older kids.

When they got home, Dad read from the Bible. He was reading from a place called First Peter, chapter 5. It was something to do about Christ, Who is the big Shepherd, and about the pastor of the church, who is the little shepherd.

Bobbie shook her head. "The man behind the big box at church was really tall. How come the Bible calls him a little shepherd?"

"It doesn't mean size. It means that Jesus Christ is the head, or the leader, of the church. The pastor is under Him."

Mom tried to help Dad explain it. She said, "The pastor reminds me of what my dad, your Grandpa Williams, does."

"Grandpa doesn't stand behind a big box and talk."

"No, but he does feed his sheep every day. He finds the best water for them and helps them when they get into trouble. In the same way the pastor of the church feeds the people good food from the Bible to help them grow to love God more and obey Him better. When the people get into trouble, he tries to help them with wise ways from the Bible. He knows that book very well."

"The people at church are sheep?" It sounded funny when Bobbie said that, but she was kind of right.

Mom told her, "Well, Bobbie, they behave like sheep and need lots of help. I'm glad that church has a good pastor."

Dad had been really quiet while Mom was talking about Grandpa and sheep, but then he said, "I think it's time I talk with that pastor about becoming a member of the church."

Bobbie asked him, "Dad, are you going to be a sheep? Will you eat grass?" That sounded even funnier.

But Dad didn't laugh. He just said, "No, Bobbie, but I'm going to talk with the shepherd and find out what I need to do to be under God's care."

Verses to Read

1 Peter 5:1–4: "The elders who are among you I exhort, Shepherd the flock of God which is among you, serving as overseers, not by compulsion but willingly, not for dishonest gain but eagerly; nor being lords over those entrusted to you, but being examples to the flock; and when the Chief Shepherd appears, you will receive the crown of glory that does not fade away" (NKJV).

QUESTIONS TO ASK YOUR CHILD
✳

1. Who is the head of the church?

2. Who is like a shepherd at church?

3. What should a pastor do?

Why Does Our Family Get Together?

Mom was kind of crabby like she always is when company is coming. She had a list on the refrigerator that had at least twenty-five "Things to Do." She told us to sign up for "five jobs each" and to have them done by lunch the next day. I knew I would be glad when our cousins finally got here. Getting ready for company isn't much fun.

Dad and I decided to take the outside jobs so that we could work together and be out of the house. We said we would mow the lawn, sweep the back porch, and pick up branches that had blown down in the windstorm the night before. Those are the boy jobs. We let the girls do the girl jobs inside—like cleaning out closets and drawers and straightening the canning jars in the basement.

I love to ride with Dad on the riding mower. It's so much fun, and it counts as work. We were halfway through mowing the backyard when Bobbie came out of the house crying. It was more fake crying than real crying. I think Bobbie does that when she wants something.

Bobbie sat down on the back porch and put her head down. Dad stopped the mower, and I went over to see if I could help.

"Bobbie, what's wrong?" I asked it as nice as I could.

"I hate company! I wish our cousins wouldn't even come!" She sure was crabby!

"Why? You've been driving us all crazy saying you can't wait until our cousins get here. Why'd you change your mind?" I was trying to be a kind big brother.

"I can't stand getting ready for them to come! I was picking up my toys and taking them to my room. My toy box was full, so I put my other toys under my bed. No one looks there but Mom." Bobbie was talking in a whiny voice.

"Let me guess. Mom came to check your work and found the toys under the bed, and she made you put them away all over again."

"How did you know?"

"I used to do that, too, when I was your age. I always got caught. Don't worry, Bobbie. Our cousins will be here before dinner tonight."

"Topher, why does our family have to get together anyway? It's too much work!"

"The cousins are coming to spend their vacation with us. I guess it's 'cause we love each other. Getting ready is kind of a pain, but it's fun when they're here. I can't wait until Trent gets here so I'll have another boy to play with. We had a blast last year when we went to their house in Atlanta for a week. They prob'ly have to get ready for us before we go there too. Anyhow, just keep thinking about how much fun it will be when they get here." Megan came out of the house too. She sat next to Bobbie.

Bobbie still seemed crabby. She told me, "Mom said we're going to their house for Christmas this year, and she said we're going again in the summer. Why do we get together so much?"

I tried to make Bobbie laugh. "Just think, they have to do the cleaning twice in a row." She finally smiled.

Then Megan answered Bobbie's question. "We get together because we love each other and want to have fun together. I guess it's kind of like that new church we visited last week. I think they must have worked hard getting ready for us to visit. They seemed like they really loved God and were happy to have visitors."

I was thinking about the church teacher. "She told us a story from the Bible, and she gave us a word puzzle to do. We had snacks and played a game and sang songs. She must have worked hard to find all that stuff to do."

Bobbie was finally not acting crabby. She smiled and said, "I'll bet God is glad when we come to visit at His house because He doesn't have to do any of the work to get ready!"

Megan nodded, but she had a funny, faraway look on her face—like her brain was far, far away. "Those people sure do seem to love God. They love Him so much that they keep His house clean and beautiful—"

"—While He's somewhere else!" Bobbie finished Megan's sentence for her.

Then I said, "I think they must love God more than we love our cousins."

Bobbie jumped up really fast. "I better finish helping Mom get ready!"

Verse to Read

Hebrews 10:25: "Not forsaking the assembling of ourselves together, as the manner of some is; but exhorting one another: and so much the more, as ye see the day approaching."

QUESTIONS TO ASK YOUR CHILD

*

1. *What is one way you can show God you love Him?*

2. *Why do people get together?*

3. *How often do you go to church to show Jesus you love Him?*

Does God Get His Children Together?

Bobbie, you must go to bed early tonight. You have ten minutes to finish building your tower." When Mom said that, she set the timer. "When the timer goes off, I want you to head for the bathroom. I'll have your bath ready for you."

"Mom! I'm not tired!" Bobbie whined. She sure sounded tired.

Mom did not sound happy. "Bobbie, you were up hours past your bedtime every night for a week while your cousins were here. You've been fussy and crabby all day, and you will go to bed early tonight. Enjoy your ten minutes, or we can begin the bath right away. Understand?"

"Yes, Mom." Finally Bobbie knew she wouldn't win. She finished her tower and actually picked up all the blocks before the timer dinged.

During her bath she asked Mom some of her famous questions. "Mom, does God ever have all of His family get together like we do?"

"What do you mean, Bobbie?" Mom asked her.

"Does God get His family together at Christmas or vacations? You said that God has a family with lots of children. Who cleans up before they get together?" Bobbie was still remembering when her family had to clean for the cousins.

Mom told her, "God's family today is called the church, and God does want them to get together often. Today people meet together at least once or twice a week. In the Bible the church met every day and ate together every day. The people were so glad to be in God's family. They met in different homes and shared food. They also had a special meal of eating bread and drinking grape juice like Jesus did the last time He ate with His disciples. The church people were the happiest people you could ever see. They loved God so much, and they liked being with each other. They got along and didn't fight at all."

"What a nice family! But who cleaned up for the guests coming? Did God have to go to bed early so He wouldn't be crabby?"

Mom answered her first question. "Actually each family probably cleaned up their home when the gathering was at their place. The believers—that's another name for them—were like one big happy family." Then Mom laughed a little. "To answer your other question, young lady—God is perfect, so He never gets crabby and doesn't need His rest like you and I do. Actually, Bobbie, thousands of people came into God's family every day at the beginning."

"Is that like zillions?"

"Well, it is more people who love God than I've ever seen in one place."

"Does God come to the parties? If all the people are in His family, does He ever come to see them? Or does He stay in Heaven and watch on TV what they're doing?"

"God sent His Son Jesus to earth for thirty-three years to live with people, die, and come alive again. He did all that so people would trust Him as Savior and be a part of His family. He can see everything that happens on the earth at once because He's everywhere at the same time. God doesn't need a TV screen to know what's going on."

"Why don't we meet every day with God's family like they did in those old days?"

Mom gave a really big sigh. "Oh, Bobbie. Save that question till later. It's time to finish up your bath and head for bed."

Verses to Read

Acts 2:41, 42, 46: "Then they that gladly received his word were baptized: and the same day there were added unto them about three thousand souls. And they continued stedfastly in the apostles' doctrine and fellowship, and in breaking of bread, and in prayers. . . . And they, continuing daily with one accord in the temple, and breaking bread from house to house, did eat their meat with gladness and singleness of heart, praising God and having favour with all the people. And the Lord added to the church daily such as should be saved."

QUESTIONS TO ASK YOUR CHILD

*

1. What is the family of God called?

2. How often does God want His family to get together?

3. Why doesn't God come to the gatherings Himself?

Why Do People Get Wet in Church?

Plese, please, please, please, can't I go too? I want to go with you to church to see the pastor." Bobbie hugged Dad's legs when he was getting his car keys and Bible. "I wanna go with you when you talk with the shepherd man. I like his voice. Please, please, please, please, can't I go with you?"

Dad thought about it for a second, and then he said okay. "But you'll have to be on your best behavior. Is that possible? This is a very important meeting. I have important questions of my own to ask Pastor, and I can't be interrupted by your questions. It's fine for you to ask questions, but right now I need to get some answers myself. What do you think?" Dad sounded like he meant it.

But Bobbie really wanted to go. "I'll be very good. I can go in the big room and sit still while you talk with Pastor. Please, Dad?"

Dad peeled Bobbie off his legs. "Okay. Get your shoes on, and let's go. I'm supposed to be there in five minutes."

When they got to church, Dad took Bobbie to the big room with

the piano and organ. It's called the auditorium. Dad told Bobbie to wait for him there. She saw Dad and Pastor walk into a room down the hall. Then she went inside the auditorium. It looked super big without any people in it. She sat down and pulled a songbook from the rack. Then she pretended to sing a song. She does that at home too. She's so silly.

Splish-splash! Bobbie heard a funny noise coming from the front of the room. She slid down low in the seat so no one could see her. It sounded like water running really fast, and she heard a man singing.

Bobbie peeked over the edge of the seat. She saw a man standing behind the box that Pastor talks from. Then he turned and stuck his head in a big window-thing in the wall. He was wearing work clothes, and he seemed to be very busy working with the water. Bobbie was a little scared, so she got up and tiptoed out of the room. She sat on a chair outside the door where she had seen Dad go in with Pastor, and just a minute later Dad and Pastor came out of the room and shook hands.

On the way home, Bobbie asked Dad about the man. "Dad, was that man getting ready to take a bath?"

Dad smiled at that question. "That was the janitor, Bobbie. He was checking the baptistry so it will be ready for me."

"For you? But we have a bathtub at home. You can take a bath there."

Then Dad tried to explain. "Bobbie, it's not a bathtub, although it does hold water in it. It's a tank used in church services when people want to tell others that they are followers of Jesus. It's like a ballplayer wearing a uniform that tells other people which team he plays for. That's what I wanted to talk to Pastor about today. I have decided to admit that I need Jesus as my Savior. I did that today with Pastor while you were in the auditorium. On Sunday I'm going to be baptized to tell everyone that I'm a follower of Jesus. That man was getting the tank ready for me."

"So it's for telling people that you love Jesus? How come you can't just say it? Why do you have to get all wet in church, Dad? Will you wear your swimming suit?"

"Whoa, little girl. One question at a time. The Bible way of telling people that you belong to Jesus is to be baptized, or completely covered with water. Baptism shows how Jesus died, was buried, and then came back to life again. When Pastor lowers me into the water, that will show how Jesus was crucified, or that He died. Then when I'm under the water, that will show how Jesus was buried; and when Pastor brings me out of the water, it will show that Jesus came back to life three days after He died and was buried. Does that make sense?"

Bobbie just nodded, so Dad went on. "I'll wear a robe over my clothes. Several others will be baptized at the same time."

"Are some of them children, Dad? Are there other dads or moms? Any grandmas or grandpas?"

"Yes, some children are being baptized, one other mom and dad, and Mrs. Jenkins. The service will be on Sunday. That's in three days."

Bobbie leaned over and patted Dad's leg. "Dad, I am so happy!"

Verses to Read

Acts 2:41: "Then they that gladly received his word were baptized: and the same day there were added unto them about three thousand souls."

Acts 16:30, 31 and 33: "Sirs, what must I do to be saved? So they said, Believe on the Lord Jesus Christ, and you will be saved, you and your household. . . . And immediately he and all his family were baptized" (NKJV).

QUESTIONS TO ASK YOUR CHILD

1. What does being baptized tell people?

2. How does baptism show what Jesus did for you?

3. If you are saved, have you been baptized?

Why Do They Sing So Much in Church?

Megan was practicing a song on the piano for the 100th time in one morning. It was an easy song, and it sounded sort of pretty—I guess. Megan was going to play for church on Sunday night, and she wanted to have the song perfect. It was the first time she had ever played in front of that many people. Mom said Megan should do her best for God, but Bobbie and I got tired of listening to the same song over and over. "Can't you play anything else? I used to like that song, but I can hear it in my sleep." And I was

serious! I really wanted her to stop playing that song!

"Turn the page, Megan. I don't like that music anymore. My ears are tired." Bobbie said that a little nicer than I did, but I know she was really sick of the music too. Then Bobbie asked Mom, "Why do we have so much music at church? We sing more than anything else. Does God like music? Does He get tired of hearing us sing?"

"Those are good questions, Bobbie. I'm just not sure how to answer them. Maybe the choir director could help us, or—I know—let's try to find the answer ourselves."

"How?"

"Get your Bible, and let's look in the back in the concordance for the word 'sing' or 'music.' That way we can find out what the Bible says about making music. I'd like to know too."

"What's a condolence?" Every time Bobbie gets her words mixed up, I laugh at her. I can't help it. It's funny.

"It's 'concordance,' Bobbie, not 'condolence.' A concordance is an easy way to find where things are. Condolence is help for someone who feels sad."

That sounded good to me. "I need condolence with Megan playing that song so much. Make her stop, Mom, please!"

But Mom was already looking in Bobbie's Bible. "Here it is under 'song.'"

"The book of Job says, 'Now am I their song. . . .'[1] God is the One we are to sing about. The Bible says that God gives songs in the night.[2] That means He helps us to sing even in times of trouble. The book of Psalms uses the word 'song' a lot. The Bible tells us to sing unto the Lord, so we sing to Him and about Him. It sounds to me like God wants us to sing."

Bobbie didn't say anything for a minute. I think she was listening to Megan play her song—AGAIN—because then she said, "I think God must get tired of the same song over and over again."

Mom smiled at Bobbie and at me. "Well, actually, I think God enjoys even the same song over and over because He knows the person is singing or playing an instrument for Him. He enjoys when we do our very best. I guess you'll have to be patient a little longer with Megan and her practicing. Maybe you and Topher can find a song of your own to sing in the basement or out on the porch so your ears can get a little rest."

Verse to Read

Colossians 3:16: "Let the word of Christ dwell in you richly in all wisdom; teaching and admonishing one another in psalms and hymns and spiritual songs, singing with grace in your hearts to the Lord."

1. Job 30:9
2. Job 35:10

QUESTIONS TO ASK YOUR CHILD
✳

1. Can you name one book of the Bible that says you should sing?

2. Who should you sing about?

3. Why should you do your best when you sing?

Why Is Church So Much like School?

The night Dad was baptized was a big night at our house. Grandma and Grandpa Williams came all the way from Pennsylvania. Megan, Bobbie, and I wore our best clothes. Mom seemed sad or happy—I couldn't tell which because she kept crying.

After the service when Dad and the others got baptized, we went to a place in the back of the church. I had never been in that part of the church before. We walked in a long hallway. Bobbie and I were kind of walking behind everyone else.

Bobbie was looking all around. "This seems like a school. Can I look in this room, Toph?"

"I guess so. But don't take too long, or we'll get lost and never find Mom and Dad."

"Look, Topher! This room has chalkboards and pictures. The chairs and tables are little for kids like me! And there's cans of pencils and crayons. It looks like preschool. Can I go?"

I told her I didn't know. When we went back to the hallway, Bobbie kept talking about it. "I wanna go to school. Mom says I have to wait. I'm going to go to kindergarten when it's school time, but I wanna go now."

I just laughed. "You wouldn't think it was so much fun if you had to go to school every day of your life, Bobbie. You can go for me if you want to. I'll give you my lunch box and backpack. You'll change your mind."

I saw Dad, Grandpa, Mom, Grandma, and Megan go inside a big room, so Bobbie and I ran to catch up with them. The room had two tables full of food and lots of chairs in circles. Bobbie told me she wanted to talk to Mom and Dad. She said she had some questions. What else is new? But Mom and Dad were talking to other people and hugging people they didn't even know. Grandpa and Grandma and Megan were doing it too! I wanted to get away from there so nobody I didn't know would hug me. I don't even like people I know hugging me.

We had to stand in line behind some people and pick up a plate and napkin like they were doing. Then we piled the plate with six kinds of fancy cookies. We got some punch too.

We followed the people to one of the circles of chairs. The people looked nice. They were very old—like Grandpa and Grandma. They sat down and started eating their cake, so Bobbie and I sat down too. I looked around at the people, and then I whispered to Bobbie, "You could ask them your questions. They look nice."

She didn't waste a second. "Hi! I'm Bobbie Schmidt. That's my dad over there. He's the one with the wet hair. He got dunked tonight. Do you have a school here? How old do you have to be to go to it? Can I come?" What a sister! She couldn't ask just one question.

The lady smiled though. "Well, honey, I'm glad to meet you. We're

Mr. and Mrs. Corbett. Mr. Corbett used to be the pastor here, but now we're retired and just helping out when we can. We do have classes here for children and adults of all ages. If you're alive, we have a class for you! We even have a class for old people like us! We meet on Sunday morning before the big service when everyone gets together in the auditorium."

Mrs. Corbett stopped to take a bite of food, and Bobbie just kept staring at her. I guess she wanted to know more, so Mrs. Corbett swallowed and kept talking. "We also have special classes in the summer when school is out. They're called Vacation Bible School. In fact, they start tomorrow morning. Perhaps your mom would let you come. I could pick you and your brother up and bring you. Don't you also have a sister who played a song on the piano tonight? Megan is her name, if I recall it."

Mrs. Corbett seemed nice enough. She remembered Megan's name, so I answered her, "We do have a sister named Megan. My mom would probably let Bobbie come to summer school at church, but I don't think I would like it. School's hard for me. I don't want to go in the summer! I don't want to do anything that's even a little like school. Besides, I'm pretty old to learn stuff at church." I was trying to be polite.

"Well, young man, you're never too old to learn more about God, and once you know a lot, you're ready to help others learn what you know. I enjoy helping others learn about God. You might change your mind if you knew all that goes on here. We have a Bible story and refreshments and games outside with our youth pastor. There are prizes, and most kids like it even if they don't like school school."

Bobbie got real excited then. "I'll come! I'll come! Do we learn about God too? Do we sing? Do they have big crayons and fat pencils?

Does the big-little shepherd come? Please ask my mom if I can come."

I wasn't really excited, but it didn't sound so bad. "Are you sure there are no report cards? They don't do math, do they? I'm really bad at math. Maybe I could come one day and see if I like it. I don't have to go, do I?"

Mrs. Corbett shook her head. "No, Son, you don't have to come, but we have hundreds of kids who love it and come back every day and bring friends with them. I promise you there are no report cards, but what you learn is so much more important than anything you could ever learn in school. It will help you all your life—and in the next life too!" Mrs. Corbett made it sound good.

"I don't know much about God or the Bible, but if you're sure there are no report cards, maybe I will give it a try."

Verse to Read

Acts 2:42: "And they continued stedfastly in the apostles' doctrine and fellowship, and in breaking of bread, and in prayers."

QUESTIONS TO ASK YOUR CHILD

1. Will you ever be too old to learn more about God?

2. What should you do after you learn about God?

3. Why is church school so important?

Why Are They Eating in Church?

Megan shouted from the kitchen, "Mom, Topher is going to the living room with his potato chips and soda!"

Toph shouted back. "I am not!"

"You are too! I can see you getting ready to sit down on the couch. You know Mom doesn't want you in there with food. You're sloppy, and you spill stuff, Toph."

"Mind your own business, Megan. I'm going out to the back porch. I was just getting my baseball magazine from the end table."

Megan and Toph argue sometimes. That's what brothers and sisters do. Megan watches everyone. She makes sure no one eats food anywhere in the house except in the kitchen or the dining room.

Later Megan tattled again. "Mom, Bobbie's taking her cereal bowl into the family room to watch cartoons while she eats."

Bobbie tried to whisper, but whenever she whispers, everyone can hear. "Shhhh, Megan! I won't spill it. Don't tell Mom. She'll make me go back to the kitchen, and I'll miss 'Mighty Dog' and 'Super Cat' on TV."

"Megan! Please come here for a minute," Mom called from upstairs. Megan smiled a silly smile at Bobbie and Toph. She thought Mom was going to thank her for telling on the others.

Boy was she surprised at what Mom told her! "Megan, I appreciate your trying to help your brother and sister remember the family rule about eating only in the dining room and kitchen, but I am tired of the tattletale voice you use to tell on the others. Please mind your own business, and I will deal with your brother and sister. Do you understand?"

Megan stopped smiling then and quietly told Mom, "I'm sorry."

In the car on the way to church the next Sunday, Mom gave a speech about not chewing gum in church. "It isn't polite to chew gum in church. This is the place to worship God, and smacking on gum just isn't proper behavior. I want all of you to spit out your gum in the rest room before the service."

Toph didn't like that rule. "But, Mom! This is a new stick of gum, and I don't have any more left. Can't I just hold it still in my mouth?"

Mom didn't go for that idea. "No, Topher, I want it out of your mouth. Do you have the wrapper? Maybe we could save it that way till after church."

They got to church a little late, so they sat in the next-to-the-back row. Bobbie sat next to Dad in case she had a question. He was the best at answering them. "Dad, why is there a white sheet on that table up front by Pastor? Is someone sleeping under there? He'll wake up and see everyone watching him!" Bobbie giggled. She was thinking about that person waking up in his pajamas in front of the church.

But Dad explained. "No, honey, that's the communion table covering. The sheet is covering trays of bread and tiny cups of juice for a special service later."

"Are people going to eat in church? Mom won't even let us chew gum. What will God think? I thought we weren't supposed to eat in church!" Bobbie was afraid to do something wrong.

"Oh, it's okay. We're supposed to be having this meal in church, Bobbie. When Jesus had His last meal with His disciples, He told them to do this often to remember what happened to Him that night and the next few days.[1] When the church was begun, people met in homes, and it was natural to eat together. Now we meet in bigger buildings, and it does seem a little different to have food here."

Bobbie seemed to understand what Dad was saying since she thought of new questions. "What happened to Jesus that next few days? Was it fun? Was it good?"

Dad was glad they were sitting in the back so he could explain to Bobbie about the Lord's Table, or communion. "Well actually, after that special dinner with His friends, Jesus went to court, and the judge found Him guilty. Then He was killed. He hurt a whole lot. He bled and died on the cross for our sins. Then another friend who was rich and a man named Nicodemus got permission to bury Him."[2]

"I don't want to remember that! It sounds very sad!"

"Bobbie, it was necessary, and Jesus didn't stay dead. In three days He came back alive again! That was the happy day! But if He didn't die, our sins couldn't be forgiven. Jesus was the only One Who could take the punishment for us. It was a sad but happy day when Jesus died for our sins and took them away."

"Oh." Bobbie stared at the food for a second. "Can I eat in church, too, Dad?"

"Bobbie, first you need to trust Jesus as your Savior, and then you should be baptized like I was. Eating this meal is only for people in the family of God. It's a special time to remember what Jesus did for you. Mom and I are going to eat today. You watch, and we can talk more at home, but, Bobbie, you may hold my bread and juice until I need to eat them."

Bobbie took the bread from Dad and smiled at him. "Someday I'll eat in church too," she whispered.

Verses to Read

1 Corinthians 11:23–29. This passage describes a service in which the Lord's Supper is observed.

1. Luke 22:17–20; 1 Corinthians 11:26
2. Matthew 27:57–61; John 19:38–42

QUESTIONS TO ASK YOUR CHILD

1. *What happened to Jesus after the special dinner with His friends?*

2. *Why do people eat bread and drink juice in church?*

3. *What do you have to do before you can eat the special meal at church?*

Who Helps the Shepherd?

Right before school started again, I got to go on my most awesome adventure ever. I did it all by myself! I flew on an airplane for my first time ever, and I spent two weeks at Grandpa and Grandma Williams' farm—all by myself.

Being on the plane was great! A flight attendant fastened my seat belt. While I waited for the plane to take off, I looked in the pocket in front of me. I found a magazine with pictures in it.

When the plane took off, I felt a little sick in my stomach, but I chewed some gum Mom had given me. At first, I chewed so hard I thought my jaw would crack in two.

Finally we were off the ground. The roads looked like pretend roads that I build in the sandbox, and the houses looked like the little buildings on my miniature railroad. The cars and trucks looked like the cars I use on my roadway cloth.

At first I was a little scared, but then it was fun. It didn't last very long though. I didn't really want it to end, but I was excited about seeing Grandpa and Grandma. The pilot told us to buckle our seat belts again because the plane was getting ready to land. When I looked out the window, I could see things that looked like my railroad and roadway cloth again.

Grandma and Grandpa were at the airport to meet me, and they got my suitcase off the conveyor belt. I learned that word "conveyor belt" from the lady standing next to us at the airport. She was waiting for her suitcases too.

The reason I got to fly to Pennsylvania was so I could help Grandpa with the sheep for the rest of the summer. Grandpa's knees were bothering him.

The next morning, before the sun was even up, Grandpa came into my room. "Rise and shine, young man. There's work to be done!" Grandpa's always cheerful in the morning. I was still sleeping and dreaming about my plane ride to Pennsylvania. I didn't want to get up at first.

But by the time I got dressed and went to the kitchen to eat, I was excited! "How many sheep are there, Grandpa? Where do we start? What can I do to help?"

"You're sounding like your little sister with so many questions, young man!" Grandpa teased me. "I had sixty sheep last year and then twenty more lambs born this spring, so that makes eighty altogether. Fill that jug with water from the hose, and we'll haul water out to the fields for the young ones. I'm so glad to have help. This work is getting to be too much for me. Thanks for coming to help, Son."

Mom and Dad called that night. They talked to me first and then to Grandpa and Grandma. Then they let me talk to Bobbie and Megan. "Bobbie, it's awesome! We hauled water to the sheep. The baby lambs are so cute. I chased down two sheep that needed to see the vet and got them into the little trailer for Grandpa. We went

swimming in the lake, and tonight we're going for ice cream. Next week is another fair, and I get to help show the animals. Grandpa is hoping to get a good price for them. Grandpa calls me his little shepherd. I miss you." I was hurrying to tell her everything I could think of.

I'm afraid I got Bobbie confused. "You're Grandpa's little shepherd, Toph? Is Grandpa the big shepherd? Do you stand in front of the sheep and hold a big book?" Bobbie was mixing things up with what Mom and Dad had told her about the pastor at church.

"No, Bobbie, you're all confused. I'm the shepherd's helper. I don't talk to the sheep. I feed them water and grain, and I help the sick ones. I'm Grandpa's extra pair of knees since his knees aren't feeling very strong. The doctor says he shouldn't work so hard anymore. Grandpa calls me his deacon. I'm not sure what that means, but maybe Dad knows. I gotta go now."

Bobbie gave the phone to Megan so she could talk to me. Then I guess Bobbie asked Dad, "What's a deacon? Why does Grandpa call

Topher a deacon? Do deacons take care of the sheep?"

"Well, the Bible says a deacon is a man who helps the pastor take care of the sheep in the church.[1] Actually a deacon is a pastor's helper who does things to help the people in the church grow and love God more. Grandpa is teasing because Topher is really just helping with the animals, but Grandpa is comparing Topher to a special helper in the church."

Those two weeks were the best two weeks of my life! I learned tons about sheep: how to know if they're sick, what to do if they're sick, how to help them get better, what they eat, how to rescue them when they get caught in the fence or escape to a neighbor's field. And maybe some day I'll be a deacon in the church. I liked taking care of sheep.

Verses to Read

1 Timothy 3:8, 9, 12: "Likewise deacons must be reverent, not double-tongued, not given to much wine, not greedy for money, holding the mystery of the faith with a pure conscience. . . . Let deacons be the husbands of one wife, ruling their children and their own houses well" (NKJV).

1. Acts 6:1–4

QUESTIONS TO ASK YOUR CHILD
✳

1. What is a deacon?

2. How does a deacon help a pastor?

Why Do They Pass the Fancy Frisbees?

One day after Toph got back from his trip to Grandpa and Grandma's, he and Bobbie picked up empty soda cans from the side of the road. They asked Megan to come too, but she was practicing her next song for church. Picking up cans is a great thing! Bobbie and Toph cleaned the road and got some money from recycling the cans, but most of all, they got out of the house when Megan was going to practice her song a hundred times.

Bobbie carried the trash bag, and Toph picked up the cans and threw them in. They made a pretty good team and had fun too. "Seventy-five, seventy-six, seventy-seven." Toph counted every can they put in the bag.

Later on, Dad took Bobbie and Toph to the recycling place to get their money. All together they had collected 150 cans. That would be 50 cents for each of them. Bobbie asked the recycling lady to give her the money in nickels so she could have more money. Toph got five dimes. Since his money was smaller, Bobbie thought she had more money than Toph.

On Sunday Toph put his money in his pants pocket. The money sounded great when it rubbed together. He wanted to spend his 50 cents on baseball cards next Saturday when Mom went shopping. That's the only time Toph likes to go shopping with Mom—when he has money for cards or when they go to the mall in Eastman.

Bobbie put her money in the purse Megan had given her for her birthday. Bobbie liked the sound her nickels made when they bumped each other.

The Schmidts had been going to Sunday School and church every week for a while. Bobbie loved going to "church school." That's what she called it. Megan and Toph liked it more all the time. After Sunday School they went to the auditorium and sat with Mom and Dad. After they had sung a song, Bobbie noticed the Pastor give some men four shiny silver plates. After Pastor prayed, Bobbie asked, "What are those shiny Frisbees, Dad?" Bobbie had never noticed them before.

Dad told her that they're offering plates. "The ushers pass them around so people can give a gift to God. Here come the ushers now."

Mom tapped Bobbie on the leg and asked, "Bobbie, do you and Topher have your money with you?" Bobbie got her money out of her

purse and showed Mom. Then Mom told her, "Trade Topher two of your nickels for one of his dimes, please." Mom was whispering so the people around the family wouldn't hear her and look at them the way they did sometimes when Bobbie asked a question.

Bobbie didn't seem to like Mom's idea. "But, Mom, then Topher will have more money than I do!" She didn't really understand money. She thought that the bigger money was better.

Mom just whispered back, "Don't argue with me, Bobbie. It's fair. I'll tell you about it later. When the offering plate comes by, Topher and Bobbie, both of you put one nickel in."

"But, Mom, it's my money. Who gets it if I put it in the Frisbee?"

Mom tried to explain a little. "It's for Pastor and to buy papers and crayons for your Sunday School class. Hurry with your money, or the offering will pass you by."

Bobbie started to pout. "Why can't Pastor make his own money? Why does he have to have mine? I'm poor." People were looking and smiling. They could hear everything Bobbie said.

Mom gave up and decided to wait to explain it. "Never mind, Bobbie," she said. "I'll talk to you later. Please be quiet."

At home Mom told Bobbie, Megan, and Toph about sharing part of what you have with God as a gift. "Giving is a way of telling God how much you love Him."

"Could I just tell God I love Him and keep my money?" Bobbie really liked her money.

"Actually, Bobbie, everything you have belongs to God. What if He decided to tell you He loved you and never gave you anything? You would have no air to breathe, no grass to play in, no bed to sleep in, no mom or dad, and certainly no money of your own."

"Everything belongs to God? Oh—" Bobbie was quiet for a little bit. Then she finally said, "Okay. How much do I have to give Him?"

"You don't have to give Him anything, but in Bible times people usually gave God one penny out of every ten pennies that they had. I want you to think about how much you love God and how much money you would like to give next Sunday in the offering."

Verses to Read

The Bible mentions a generous church that was willing to give to the needs of the poorer saints in Jerusalem. Read more about it in 1 Corinthians 16:1–3, where Paul gives instructions about when to give, how often, and with what attitude.

1 Corinthians 16:1–3: "Now concerning the collection for the saints, as I have given order to the churches of Galatia, even so do ye. Upon the first day of the week let every one of you lay by him in store, as God hath prospered him, that there be no gatherings when I come. And when I come, whomsoever ye shall approve by your letters, them will I send to bring your liberality unto Jerusalem."

QUESTIONS TO ASK YOUR CHILD

✳

1. Why do churches have offering plates?

2. What is the money used for?

3. How much should you give to God?

Kids' Questions about the Future

Hints and Helps

Do you like to know what is ahead as you travel down a road? Signs help adults, but children, whether they can read or not, often ignore signs and prefer another method of finding out what they want to know. When kids are young, they ask the universal question, "Are we there yet?" And parents give the universal answer, "Not yet; be patient."

Even adults want to know where they are going—figuratively as well as literally. Chicago has special financial institutions called futures markets. New York City is home of the New York Stock Exchange, the stock market where people buy and sell shares in various companies. They buy and sell based on a company's present condition and on their own judgment about the company's future. We are all interested in the future.

At every age throughout childhood, we wished that we were older and that the future would arrive more quickly. When we were in kindergarten, we longed for first grade. When we were in junior high, we could not wait until high school, and when we were in high school, we longed for graduation.

The Bible has a lot to say about the future. A number of Bible books reveal a great deal about the future. Important ones are Daniel,

Isaiah, and Revelation, although we can find many other Bible references concerning the future. Jesus talked a lot about the future. He told His disciples that He was going to Heaven to prepare a place for them so that when they died, they could be with Him (John 14:1–3).

Each of us has a body, which is the outer man, and a soul and spirit, which is the inner man. At death, a Christian's physical body goes into the grave, but the inner man goes to Heaven (2 Corinthians 5:6–8). At the resurrection, the Christian's body will be resurrected and will go to Heaven to be reunited with the inner man. At that same time the living saints will be raptured, or taken up, by transformation without death (1 Thessalonians 4:13–18).

The Bible reveals much more about the future, but we should note one of the important facts: the Bible teaches that Christ will someday rule over everyone and everything with His Father in Heaven (1 John 3:1–3; Revelation 22:12–17).

Verse to Memorize

Acts 1:11: "This same Jesus, which is taken up from you into heaven, shall so come in like manner as ye have seen him go into heaven."

What Happens to People When They Die?

I **get the window!**" I called that to Megan and Bobbie as they got into the car. I still had to finish packing my backpack for the trip to Atlanta, but when I got to the car, Megan was sitting by one window, and Bobbie had taken the other one. I asked Bobbie to move to the middle so I could get in the car. She wouldn't move. I started to make her move, but Mom came out then.

"Children, you'll have to take turns. Topher let the girls take the windows until we stop next time for gasoline. Then you can trade with one of them. Does that sound fair?" Mom always tries to find a solution that makes everyone happy.

This time I mumbled, "Sure." Then I had to crawl over Bobbie to get to my seat.

Just after we got out of town, Mom said she had an idea. She was really trying to keep everyone happy. "Why don't we play the cow game? You count all the cows or horses on your side of the road. The first one to 100 wins. If you pass a cemetery, you lose all your points and have to start over again. Everybody understand the rules?"

I looked out Bobbie's window, since I could see over her head. "I got ten over there in that pasture." I was the first one to score. "I have seven here." Megan scored next.

"I don't have any! I can't play because there are no more sides of the road." I think Bobbie was feeling sorry for herself because I beat her in counting the cows. She's only four, and she can't count very fast.

Mom tried to make her feel better. "Don't give up easily, Bobbie. Keep your eyes open, and you'll score soon. How about if we changed the game, and you get to count sheep on both sides of the road? What do you think?" Mom was full of ideas.

"Uh-huh. That's a good idea." Bobbie was happier after that. "Eighty-eight, eighty-nine, ninety! I'm going to win." I was way ahead of the others.

Just then Megan spotted a cemetery on my side of the road. "See that cemetery by the little church up there on the hill? Ha! You lose all your points."

"I don't see it. You made that up, Megan. I have ninety-five points now." I did think maybe I saw a cemetery, but I wasn't going to tell Megan I did. She would have won.

Mom solved the problem again. "I did see the cemetery, Topher, and, Megan, you lose ten points for pointing out someone else's cemetery. Watch on your own side of the road."

Bobbie had a question. "What's a cemetery? And how come it makes Topher lose all his points?" Even with looking out both windows, Bobbie wasn't getting many points, but she was thinking of lots of questions.

I could answer that one. "A cemetery is for dead people, Bobbie. It's where you put the bodies after people quit breathing. It's like bad luck. That's why you lose all your points."

Bobbie looked a little scared. "When I fell off my tricycle last week, I quit breathing, and you didn't put me into a cemetery."

Mom had to help me explain better. "Cemeteries are for people whose hearts have stopped beating and who have stopped breathing forever. There is no life left in them. It's what happened to Grandma Jenkins from church last week. She was very old. Her heart quit, and she stopped breathing."

Then we got more questions. "Do people stay there for long? Does it hurt to be in a cemetery? Why do they have those stones? I don't want to be in a cemetery. It sounds really yucky."

Mom had more answers. "It's only your body that is buried in the cemetery. You can't feel anything when you're dead. Your body is there, but the real you inside goes to Heaven if you love Jesus. The stone is there so that people can know where each person is buried. Someday when Jesus comes back, each body will be rejoined with its person and live in Heaven forever—if that person loves Jesus."

Megan stopped counting cows for a second and said, "Then a cemetery isn't bad luck. If you love Jesus, it's a place for your body to wait for Him."

"Cemeteries are nice. I think we should get ten extra points when we see a cemetery!" And for once Bobbie had a really good idea.

Verse to Memorize

Hebrews 9:27: "And as it is appointed unto men once to die, but after this the judgment."

QUESTIONS TO ASK YOUR CHILD

1. What is buried in a cemetery?

2. What happens to a person who loves Jesus when he dies?

3. When Jesus comes back, what will happen to those who have died and loved Jesus?

Will God Have a Family Reunion?

"Mom, will you show me these pictures?" Bobbie had been in the basement. She came upstairs with a photo album from when Mom was a girl. "Who are these people? Do you know them?"

Mom stopped doing the dishes. "Come over to the couch and sit down with me, Bobbie. I haven't seen this album for a long time." She opened the book. "Oh my, that's Aunt Ruth. She was a dear woman who really loved God. Here is Uncle Clyde. He was killed in a car accident when I was just a little girl. My mom told me that Uncle Clyde loved Jesus when he was a boy and made a decision at camp to become a Christian."

"Where is Uncle Clyde now, Mom? Is he with Jesus in Heaven?" That was an important question. Sometimes Bobbie does ask big things.

Mom nodded. "Yes, Bobbie. I believe Uncle Clyde is with Jesus. My mom had a very large family, and each of them loved the Lord. Most of them aren't alive anymore."

Bobbie stared at the picture of Uncle Clyde. Her nose almost touched the page. "Did you ever have all your family together? Does God ever get all of His family together and have a family renoonon like we had in Texas last year for Dad's family?"

"That's 'reunion,' honey." Mom hugged Bobbie. "I love you, Bobbie. I love your questions. You often ask the most important questions of the day! Now let's see about answers. I have never met Aunt Ginny, Uncle Jim, or Grandma Van Allen. They were all with Jesus before I was born. I know them from pictures but not face-to-face. We try to get together as often as we can, but we're such a large family it's hard with all the work schedules. And now our family has moved around and lives farther apart. I have cousins from California to Vermont, Wisconsin to Texas. What else did you ask?" Mom tried to remember, but Bobbie had asked so many questions at the same time.

"Does God ever get all His family together? He must have tons of aunts and uncles."

"Bobbie, God has children only, no grandchildren and no aunts or uncles. No one else lived before God, so no one in the world is older or smarter than He is, but He does have many sons and daughters, people who have accepted the free gift of payment for sin that Jesus provided when He died on the cross."

"Okay. Just sons and daughters. So do they ever get all together for a renoo—"

"Reunion." Mom and Bobbie said it slowly together.

"Well, like my family, some have already died and gone to Heaven to be with Jesus forever. Many are still alive, but they live all around the world. Everywhere that people live, God has some sons and daughters. The Bible says God is building a family from every tribe and tongue and nation under the sun.[1] God has others who will be in His family who are not even born yet."

"How does He build a family from tongues, Mom?" Bobbie took it just like it sounded, but Mom didn't really mean building from tongues.

Mom tried to explain it. "It means people from every different language spoken on earth. It really means people from everywhere."

"So why doesn't it say that? Why do they make it hard?" Bobbie was quiet for a little bit. She thought about the people from everywhere trying to get together for a reunion. Then she asked, "So for some people, it would be too far to travel to a reunion?"

Mom nodded again. "Yes, but someday Jesus is coming back in the clouds to give everybody a free ride to Heaven so that He can have all His family together. It will be better than being an astronaut or a jet pilot. The Bible says that those who died loving Jesus will go to the reunion first, then those who are still alive on the earth will go next, and all of us who love Jesus will meet Him in the air. We will get to be with Him forever."[2]

"How will we get there? in planes? big balloons? rockets?"

"We'll get there without any kind of traveling machine. Jesus will just take those who love Him. We will just go up in the air—"

Bobbie started jumping up and down, over and over. Mom asked her, "What are you doing?"

Bobbie looked at Mom like Mom was supposed to know what Bobbie was doing. "Mom! I'm getting ready for the reunion."

Verses to Read

John 17:20–23: "Neither pray I for these alone, but for them also which shall believe on me through their word; that they all may be one; as thou, Father, art in me, and I in thee, that they also may be one in us: that the world may believe that thou hast sent me. And the glory which thou gavest me I have given them; that they may be one, even as we are one: I in them, and thou in me, that they may be made perfect in one."

This is the prayer that Jesus prayed for those who are in His family— past, present, and future. For a description of the reunion in the sky, read 1 Thessalonians 4:13–18.

1. Revelation 5:9
2. 1 Thessalonians 4:13–17

QUESTIONS TO ASK YOUR CHILD

*

1. *What kind of family does God have?*

2. *When will all of God's family be together?*

3. *Are you a part of God's family?*

What If You Miss the Family Reunion?

I'll name the player, and you tell me what basketball team he played for. Okay, Bobbie?"

"Topher, I don't like this game. It's too hard. Can't we do something else?" Bobbie doesn't like it when Toph pretends she is his little brother, but he wants her to know all the important basketball facts. That way when his friends come over, he can show them how smart his little sister is.

He practically had to beg her. "Please, Bobbie! You're getting so good. We won't do too many this time. I promise."

Finally she gave in. "Okay, only because I love you, Toph! Make the first ones easy.

"Tracy McGrady?"

"Orlando Magic."

"Right, Bobbie! Good guess! How about Eddy Curry?"

"He's for the Chicago Bullets."

Toph smiled a little, but he didn't laugh, or she would have stopped playing. "No, it's the Chicago Bulls, Bobbie, but you were close. All right, little sister. Tim Duncan?"

"San Antonio Sirs?"

Toph just smiled again. "Close! San Antonio Spurs. How about Larry Bird?"

"He played for Boston Celts."

"Yes! Okay, here's a hard one—Michael Jordan played for—?"

"Chicago Bulls! Ha! I got it! Now let's play my game. I learned it at Sunday School, and I kind of made it up. I'll say a person in the Bible, and you tell me if he's in God's family or not. Ready?"

"Oh, Bobbie, I learn some stuff in Sunday School and children's

61

church, but Mom's been reading the Bible to you since your birthday. You pro'bly know more than I do. Go easy on me, okay?"

"How about Moses? In God's family or not?"

"Yes. He was God's leader in the Old times."

"It's Old Testament." Bobbie was so pleased to know about the Bible. "You were close. How about Goliath?"

Toph just had to think for a second. "He's a bad guy, I think. I'll say he's not in the family of God."

Bobbie patted him on the back. "Good job, Topher. He was a bad giant. How about Hannah?"

Toph didn't even try to think about that one. "Hannah? I've never heard of him. Who's he?"

"It's a girl! She was Samuel's mother. She's in God's family. How about Mr. Schmidt?"

"That one I know for sure. In the family!"

"Okay. Megan Schmidt? and Topher Schmidt?"

Toph wasn't sure what to say about Megan. "We should ask Megan, but I'm sure about me! I believed on Jesus and got into God's family at Grandpa and Grandma's house last summer. I'm glad I'm in God's family. Last week in church school I learned that when Jesus comes back to take the people in His family to Heaven with Him, everyone else will get left behind. Then they're going to have a terrible time of trouble. They won't be able to find food to eat, and the bad guys will be in charge of everything!" Then Toph thought of something kind of sad and scary. He wasn't sure if Bobbie was in God's family or not. "I want you to come with us, Bobbie!"

"I want to come too, Toph. Let's go talk to Mom. I want to be in God's family too."

Verses to Read

John 3:36: "He that believeth on the Son hath everlasting life: and he that believeth not the Son shall not see life; but the wrath of God abideth on him."

Matthew 24:21: "For then shall be great tribulation, such as was not since the beginning of the world to this time, no, nor ever shall be.

QUESTIONS TO ASK YOUR CHILD

✳

1. When Jesus comes back, what happens to those who don't love Him?

2. Will you go with Jesus, or will you be left behind?

Where Will the Reunion Meet?

I know the Cleveland Browns aren't the greatest team, but we live near Cleveland, and everybody there loves the Browns. It doesn't matter if the Browns are good or bad or just okay; we love the Browns. This fall I had my next-best most awesome adventure. Dad and I went to a real National Football League game! We got to see the Browns play up close!

When Dad and I were getting ready to leave, Mom was fussing over me as if I were a little kid and not almost nine years old. "Here, put on another shirt, and carry these two sweatshirts. I know best, and the more layers you have on, the warmer you'll be. It's supposed to be in the 30s today at the stadium. Don't forget your hooded sweatshirt. You'll be glad you have it."

Finally Dad and I got in the car and left. I asked questions the whole way. I think it was because I was so excited. Dad laughed and said I sounded like Bobbie. Yuck!

After we parked our car and walked to the stadium, I hardly said anything. I had never seen so many people at the same time. I was kind of afraid a few times because I thought I couldn't see Dad. I was afraid I'd get lost and never be found, so I stayed as close to Dad as I could. I felt a lot better when we found our seats and sat down.

The game was a close one. Dad and I cheered until we couldn't even talk. We lost our voices. It was a good thing we cheered so hard because it helped the Browns win. That was a great day for football!

On our way home, I got to wondering about all those people. I asked Dad, "When we get to Heaven, will there be as many people as there were at the game today?"

"Topher, that's a great question. Maybe Bobbie's rubbing off on you." Dad laughed, and I laughed too. It was funny. Then Dad answered me. "There'll be too many people in Heaven to count, but it will seem like lots of people. Today's game had an all-time record attendance of 65,000. That's nothing compared with Heaven. There will be people from as far back as Adam and Eve through the old times and the new times and people alive today and some not yet born. It will be quite a crowd. I'm sure glad that you made certain last summer that you will be with them, Toph!"

"So am I, Dad. Where will we meet that will hold that many people? Does God have a huge stadium or something for us all to meet in?"

Dad smiled. "Well, I've learned from the Bible that Jesus has gone to Heaven to get a place ready for all of us who love Him. It must be a very big place, because He made the earth in seven days, and He's been in Heaven getting this place ready for about 2,000 years! In John chapter 14 Jesus described the place as 'mansions.' I can't wait to see what He has ready. I've always wanted to live in a mansion. How about you, Topher?"

I did think that sounded good.

Verses to Read

John 14:2, 3: "In my Father's house are many mansions: if it were not so, I would have told you. I go to prepare a place for you. And if I go and prepare a place for you, I will come again, and receive you unto myself; that where I am, there ye may be also."

QUESTIONS TO ASK YOUR CHILD

1. What is Jesus doing in Heaven?

2. The Bible says the place will be like what?

3. Will you have a mansion in Heaven?

How Long Will We Be There?

Do we have to go to the dentist today, Mom?" Megan was scared and hoped Mom would say no. "Sorry, honey, but we're going after lunch."

"How long will we be there? I hope not long enough for me to have a turn."

Mom patted Megan on the back to help her not be scared. "Sorry, but each of you children is scheduled for a checkup today. You had better get into the bathroom to brush your teeth. I'll set the timer. I want you to brush your teeth until it goes off. Then rinse your mouth really well." Mom knows how much Megan doesn't like going to the dentist.

A few days later Toph asked Mom if they were going to the state fair this year. "I loved it when we went to the fair at Grandma and Grandpa's. We are going, aren't we?"

"Topher, we were planning to go, but now I don't know if we'll be able to go to the fair or not. Dad has to work overtime on a construction project. We may not be able to go after all."

"Mom, that's terrible! Can I go with Tommy's family if we don't go? They'd let me if you asked them. Please? Please? You know that I love the fair."

Mom didn't answer right away. It's hard when she makes him wait. She told him, "We'll have to talk with Dad, Topher. I would like for you to be able to go, but we'll have to see."

"Does that mean yes? It means yes, doesn't it, Mom!" Toph kept bugging her because he really wanted to go to the state fair.

"Be patient, Topher. Your dad and I will talk about it tonight. We'll let you know as soon as we can."

When it was still summer, Bobbie asked Mom, "When will I get to start school? How long will I get to be there?"

Mom told her to be patient too. "Bobbie, you're still too young to go to school all day. When school starts in a few weeks, you'll go to kindergarten. You'll go in the mornings and come home right before lunch, just like in preschool." Bobbie had been asking to go to school since she was really little. She went to preschool last year, and she loved it. Now she didn't want to wait even a few more weeks for kindergarten to start.

"But, Mom, you said I could go to school pretty soon. I can't wait any longer. I want to go now. I want to stay forever. I love school. Why can't you call and tell them that I'm coming? It's been forever already, Mom. I can't wait anymore." Bobbie used her most whiny voice.

Mom told her, "Bobbie, you'll have to wait whether you want to or not, and forever is a very long time. It never ends. Do you want to sleep at school and never come home for dinner? We sure will miss you here."

Bobbie thought for a little bit. Soon she said, "No, I guess I don't want to be at school forever. I love you and Dad and Topher and Megan." Then she ran up to her room. In a few minutes she came back downstairs. She had more questions. "Mom, how long will we be in Heaven? Is that forever too? Won't we ever come back home for dinner or to see Shep? Who will cut our grass while we're gone?"

"Heaven is forever, and it's going to be wonderful, Bobbie! You won't want to come back here for anything. God will take care of all of our needs. He'll feed us and give us a place to stay. I am so glad that our whole family will be there. Forever will not seem long because we will be with the One we love—Jesus! That's the best part about Heaven—Jesus is going to be there!"

Verse to Memorize

1 Thessalonians 4:17: "Then we which are alive and remain shall be caught up together with them in the clouds, to meet the Lord in the air: and so shall we ever be with the Lord."

QUESTIONS TO ASK YOUR CHILD

✳

1. How long will saved people be in Heaven?

2. What is the best thing about Heaven?

3. Are you going to Heaven?

What Will We Do in Heaven?

Megan was on the phone with her friend Kendra. They were talking about camp.

"What will we do at Camp Cayuga?" Megan asked her. "Is it like church all day for a week? I don't think I could take that much church. Have you been there before, Kendra? Is it fun? How much does it cost?"

Mom and Bobbie were baking cookies in the kitchen when Megan got off the phone. "Mom, Kendra wants to know if I can go to Camp Cayuga with her next week. Can I go?"

"What will you do there, Megan? Are there counselors? Who's the speaker? How will you get there? How much does it cost?" Mom sure asked a lot of questions.

"Mom, you sound like Bobbie! Kendra says that she had a super counselor last summer. There's one meeting in the morning and one at night. They have time for crafts, swimming, hiking, and horseback riding. There's a snack place where you can get candy and ice cream

and pop. I don't know how we get there. Kendra didn't know the cost. Maybe you could call Kendra's mom and ask your other questions. I think I really want to go. So can I? Can I?"

"It sounds interesting, Megan, but I'll need more information, and I would like to talk it over with your dad before making a decision. Would you please get Mrs. Battalgia's phone number for me? I'll call and talk to her."

Mom went to call Kendra's mom. That's when Bobbie started asking Megan questions. She'd been licking the beaters, and she hadn't been listening to everything Megan had told Mom. "Where's Camp Cay—Cayu— Camp? And what do you do there?" Bobbie asked.

Megan told her, "I think it's in the hilly part of Ohio. You do lots of fun stuff there."

"Can I go? Is it like church all day? Do you sit and listen to the little shepherd talk all the time? Do you want to go, Megan? Is camp like Heaven? Do you play on harps all day? I can't even play a harp. Maybe the angels play the harps and we just hum."

Megan and Toph laughed. They were imagining all the kids at camp wearing wings and playing harps.

When Megan stopped laughing, she answered Bobbie, "I don't know about Heaven, but camp is a lot of fun. You swim, play games, ride horses, and eat junk food. Kendra's been there, and she liked it. I think I'll like it too. Ask Mom about Heaven. I don't know what we'll do there. Hope it isn't boring 'cause we're going to be there forever, Mom says." Then Megan started talking about what she wanted to take to camp with her and how much money she could spend at the snack shack.

When Mom got off the phone, Bobbie did ask her Heaven question. "Mom, what will we do in Heaven? Will we hum while the angels play harps?" Bobbie had forgotten about camp since she couldn't go anyway. She did plan to go to Heaven someday though.

"We'll tell God how much we love Him. We'll sing. I think you'll get to sit on Jesus' lap and have Him tell you how much He loves you. We'll get to talk with people from the Bible and make friends with Moses, David, Daniel, Mary, Hannah, Rahab, and many others. We'll never get tired of it. God will see to that. We'll sing to Jesus that He is a wonderful Lamb. We won't cry there or be sad or ever go to the doctor or dentist again. We won't have night-lights because it will always be light there and because Jesus is the light. Grandpa won't need his cane anymore, because his knees won't hurt then."

"There's going to be music though, right? Maybe in Heaven God can make me a perfect piano player. I could be like Megan except never have to practice."

Verses to Read

Revelation 21:1–4: "And I saw a new heaven and a new earth: for the first heaven and the first earth were passed away; and there was no more sea.

And I John saw the holy city, new Jerusalem, coming down from God out of heaven, prepared as a bride adorned for her husband. And I heard a great voice out of heaven saying, Behold, the tabernacle of God is with men, and he will dwell with them, and they shall be his people, and God himself shall be with them, and be their God. And God shall wipe away all tears from their eyes; and there shall be no more death, neither sorrow, nor crying, neither shall there be any more pain: for the former things are passed away."

QUESTIONS TO ASK YOUR CHILD

✳

1. *Name some things that will happen in Heaven.*

2. *What will not happen in Heaven?*

3. *Who is the light in Heaven?*

Who Goes to Heaven?

Mom, Cassidy says that I can't go to Heaven because I'm a liar. Will I get to go to Heaven? I really want to." Bobbie was crying and asking questions at the same time.

"What did you say, Bobbie? What made her think that you are a liar?"

Bobbie sniffed. "I said I wasn't going to camp because I didn't want to go, but Cassidy knows I'm not old enough."

"Well, Bobbie, it's always best to tell the truth. Did you tell her you were sorry? Did you tell her you know you're too young?"

Bobbie nodded and sniffed again. "I did, Mom, but she kept saying I'm a liar and can't go to Heaven. I'm scared, Mom. I want to go to Heaven. Won't Jesus forgive me if I say I'm sorry?"

Bobbie talks about Heaven a lot. She knows that it's wonderful, that Jesus is there, that it's like a big family reunion. She knows that people who love God from as far back as Adam and all the way till now—and people not even born yet—will be there. She knows that Jesus will come in the clouds to get His special people from the cemeteries and get the ones living at that moment too. She knows that

those who aren't in God's family when Jesus takes the others will stay here on earth for a time of big trouble. Toph told her that last part.

But Bobbie wasn't sure what happens when a little girl—or someone else—does wrong things after she has asked Jesus to save her.

So she asked Mom if a little girl needs to get saved again. "What happens if someone disobeys God after God puts him into His family? Does the person still get to go to Heaven?"

Mom got out her Bible. "Bobbie, let's check this problem out. Here, I'll read to you from the book of Revelation where the Bible tells us about those who don't get to go to Heaven." She read the verse. [1] Then she had to explain the verse to Bobbie. It was a hard verse. "It says that murderers will not get to be in Heaven, and people who aren't faithful to their husbands or wives will not get to be in Heaven, and people who worship other gods and worship other things more than God will not get to be in Heaven, and people who get information about the future from worshiping Satan will not get to be in Heaven. It says that liars will not go to Heaven."

She looked down at the Bible again. "It's interesting that it also says that those who are fearful and unbelieving will find out that they, too, will not be in Heaven. I believe that it means people who lie on purpose and live all the time in those sins will not be let into Heaven. The Bible says that Satan is a liar and the father of all lies[2], so those who lie all the time will not be allowed to enter God's Heaven."

Then Bobbie looked real scared. "But Mom, I want to go to Heaven. I don't lie all the time. I asked Jesus to save me. You said He would. Is that true?"

"Yes, Bobbie, it is true. The Bible says, "For whosoever shall call upon the name of the Lord shall be saved."[3] It also says, "He is faithful and just to forgive us our sins."[4] Once we are saved, we still sin. The Bible says we need to confess those sins to God. Your part is to admit that what you said or did or thought is wrong in God's eyes."

"That's easy, Mom. I already did that part. I am sorry. I learned my lesson. I'm going to be careful about what I say. I love God. I'm going to live with Him forever!"

Verses to Read

1 Corinthians 15:3, 4: "For I delivered unto you first of all that which I also received, how that Christ died for our sins according to the scriptures; and that he was buried, and that he rose again the third day according to the scriptures."

1 John 1:9: "If we confess our sins, he is faithful and just to forgive us our sins, and to cleanse us from all unrighteousness."

Revelation 21:3, 4: "And I heard a great voice out of heaven saying, Behold, the tabernacle of God is with men, and he will dwell with them, and they shall be his people, and God himself shall be with them, and be their God. And God shall wipe away all tears from their eyes; and there shall be no more death, neither sorrow, nor crying, neither shall there be any more pain: for the former things are passed away."

1. Revelation 21:8
2. John 8:44
3. Romans 10:13
4. 1 John 1:9

QUESTIONS TO ASK YOUR CHILD
✳

1. Who will not go to Heaven?

2. How can you go to Heaven?

3. When you tell God you are sorry for your sins, what happens?

Farewell to Adult Readers

We trust you have been challenged as you and your child, grandchild, or neighbor child have learned more about the church and what lies ahead for all of us in the future. Jesus is coming back soon. He wants to be your Father and have you in His forever family. If you have not already settled that matter, you need to do so before He returns. It could be today!

God is preparing a place for our eternal residence in much the same way He made the earth for us. He wants you to live with Him forever, but He won't force you.

Jesus told His disciples right before He died that He was going to prepare a place for all those that love Him. The future seems uncertain as we face our modern world with its terrorists, bombs, suicides, and holy wars against Christianity. Jesus said, "Let not your heart be troubled: ye believe in God, believe also in me. . . . I am the way, the truth, and the life: no man cometh unto the Father, but by me (John 14:1, 6).